D0426289

Joan of Arc

Joan of Arc

In Her Own Words

Compiled and Translated by

WILLARD TRASK

Afterword by

SIR EDWARD S. CREASY

✝

B·O·O·K·S & Co.
A Turtle Point Imprint
NEW YORK

B·O·O·K·S & Co.
TURTLE POINT PRESS
New York

© 1996

Design: Christine Taylor
Composition: Wilsted & Taylor Publishing Services

Library of Congress Number 95-080863
ISBN 1-885983-08-5

Contents

Girlhood

1412–1429

AMONG MY OWN PEOPLE, I was called Jehanette; since my coming into France, I am called Jehanne.

I was born in the village of Domremy. My father's name is Jacques d'Arc, my mother's Isabelle.

As long as I lived at home, I worked at common tasks about the house, going but seldom afield with our sheep and other cattle. I learned to sew and spin: I fear no woman in Rouen at sewing and spinning.

As to my schooling, I learned my faith, and was rightly and duly taught to do as a good child should.

From my mother I learned "Our Father," "Hail Mary," and "I believe." And my teaching in my faith I had from her and from no one else.

Once a year I confessed my sins to our parish-priest, or, when he was unable, to another with his permission. And I received the sacrament of the Eucharist at Easter time.

✛

Not far from Domremy there is a tree called the Ladies'
Tree, and others call it the Fairies' Tree, and near it there
is a fountain. And I have heard that those who are sick
with fever drink at the fountain or fetch water from it,
to be made well. Indeed, I have seen them do so, but
I do not know whether it makes them well or not. I
have heard, too, that the sick, when they can get up,
go walking under the tree. It is a great tree, a beech,
and from it our fair May-branches come; and it was
in the lands of Monseigneur Pierre de Bourlemont.
Sometimes I went walking there with the other girls,
and I have made garlands under the tree for the statue
of the Blessed Virgin of Domremy.

I have often heard it said by old people (they were not
of my own elders) that the fairies met there. My god-
mother even told me that she had seen fairies there, but
I do not know whether it was true or not. I never saw
any fairies under the tree to my knowledge. I have seen
girls hang wreaths on the branches; I have sometimes
hung my own with the others, and sometimes we took
them away with us and sometimes we left them behind.

I do not know whether, after I reached years of discretion, I ever danced at the foot of the tree; I may have

danced there sometimes with the children; but I sang there more than I danced.

There is a wood in Domremy, called the Polled Wood; you can see it from my father's door, it is not half a league away. I never heard that the fairies met there. But when I was on my journey to my King, I was asked by some if there was not a wood in my country called the Polled Wood, for it had been prophesied that a maid would come from near that wood to do wonderful things. But I said I had no faith in that.

✤

After I was grown and had reached years of discretion, though I did not commonly tend the cattle, I would sometimes help take them to pasture, or to a stronghold called the Island when there was fear of soldiers.

Once, for fear of the Burgundians, I left home and went to the town of Neufchâteau in Lorraine, to the house of a woman named La Rousse, and stayed there about two weeks.

✤

When I was thirteen, I had a voice from God to help me to govern myself. The first time, I was terrified. The voice came to me about noon: it was summer, and I was in my father's garden. I had not fasted the day before. I heard the voice on my right hand, towards the church. There was a great light all about.

I vowed then to keep my virginity for as long as it should please God.

I saw it many times before I knew that it was Saint Michael. Afterwards he taught me and showed me such things that I knew that it was he.

He was not alone, but duly attended by heavenly angels. I saw them with the eyes of my body as well as I see you. And when they left me, I wept, and I wished that they might have taken me with them. And I kissed the ground where they had stood, to do them reverence.

Above all, Saint Michael told me that I must be a good child, and that God would help me. He taught me to behave rightly and to go often to church. He said that I would have to go into France.

He told me that Saint Catherine and Saint Margaret would come to me, and that I must follow their counsel; that they were appointed to guide and counsel me in what I had to do, and that I must believe what they would tell me, for it was at our Lord's command.

He told me the pitiful state of the Kingdom of France.

And he told me that I must go to succour the King of France.

Saint Catherine and Saint Margaret had rich crowns on their heads. They spoke well and fairly, and their voices are beautiful—sweet and soft.

The name by which they often named me was *Jehanne the Maid, child of God*.

They told me that my King would be restored to his Kingdom, despite his enemies. They promised to lead me to Paradise, for that was what I asked of them.

✝

Twice and thrice a week the voice told me that I must depart and go into France.

And the voice said that I would raise the siege before Orléans. And it told me to go to Vaucouleurs, to Robert de Baudricourt, captain of the town, who would give me men to go with me.

And I answered the voice that I was a poor girl who knew nothing of riding and warfare.

Departure

February, 1429

FROM THE TIME that I knew I must go into France, I gave myself little to games and frolics—as little as I could.

I did not talk of my visions—not that my voices told me to hide them but I was afraid to let them be known, for dread of the Burgundians and that they would prevent me from starting on my journey. And, even more, I feared that my father would prevent me.

My mother had told me that my father often dreamed that I would run away with a band of soldiers. That was more than two years after I first heard the voices. She told me that he had said to my brothers, "If I believed that the thing I have dreamed about her would come to pass, I would want you to drown her; and if you would not, I would drown her myself." On account of these dreams, my father and mother watched me closely and kept me in great subjection. And I was obedient in everything.

But since God had commanded me to go, I must do it. And since God had commanded it, had I had a hundred fathers and a hundred mothers, and had I been a king's daughter, I would have gone.

It pleased God thus to act through a simple maid in order to turn back the King's enemies.

I went to my uncle and told him that I would visit him for a time. I was in his house for about a week; then I told him that I must go to Vaucouleurs. And my uncle took me there.

Vaucouleurs

February, 1429

When I came to Vaucouleurs I knew Robert de Baudricourt, though I had never seen him before. The voice told me that it was he.

And I told him that I must go into France.

HER WORDS TO

ROBERT DE BAUDRICOURT

The Kingdom of France is not the Dauphin's but my Lord's. But my Lord wills that the Dauphin shall be made King and have the Kingdom in custody. The Dauphin shall be King despite his enemies, and I shall lead him to his anointing.

✟

Twice he refused and rejected me.

AT HER LODGING

TO JEAN DE METZ

I am come to this town, which is the King's, to ask Robert de Baudricourt to take me or send me to the King. And he heeds neither me nor my words. Nevertheless, I must be with the King before mid-Lent, though I wear my legs to the knees on the road. For there is none in this world—neither kings, nor dukes, nor the King of Scotland's daughter, nor any other—who can restore the Kingdom of France. Nor is there any succour for it but from me.

Far rather would I sit and sew beside my poor mother, for this thing is not of my condition. But I must go, and I must do this thing, because my Lord will have it so.

Rather now than tomorrow, and tomorrow than the day after!

✠

And the third time he received me and gave me men. The voice had told me that so it would come to pass.

From Vaucouleurs to Chinon

February–March, 1429

I DO NOT FEAR their soldiers; my way lies open. If there are soldiers on the road, I have my Lord with me, who will make a road for me to reach the Dauphin.

I was born for this.

✛

I set out from Vaucouleurs in men's clothing. I carried a sword that Robert de Baudricourt had given me, but no other arms. With me there were a knight, a squire, and four serving-men.

Robert de Baudricourt made those who went with me swear that they would guide me well and safely.

To me at parting he said: "Go, and, whatever may come of it, let it come!"

HER WORDS TO HER COMPANIONS

Fear not: what I do, I do by commandment. My brothers in Paradise tell me what I must do. It is four or five years since my brothers in Paradise and my Lord first told me that I must go to war to restore the Kingdom of France.

✝

I met no hindrance on my journey to the King.

We reached Saint Urbain and spent the night in the abbey. We passed through Auxerre and heard mass in the great church. My voices were with me often.

When we came to Sainte-Catherine-de-Fierbois I sent a letter to my King to ask if I might enter the town where he was. It said that I had travelled a hundred and fifty leagues to come to him with help, and that I knew many things which would profit him. I heard three masses in one day there; then I went on to Chinon, where the King was.

I came to Chinon about noon and put up at an inn, and, after dinner, I went to the King in his castle. And when I entered the King's chamber, I knew him among the rest, for the voice counselled me and revealed it to me. And I told the King that I would go to make war on the English.

HER WORDS TO CHARLES

I bring you news from God, that our Lord will give you back your kingdom, bringing you to be crowned at Reims, and driving out your enemies. In this I am God's messenger. Do you set me bravely to work, and I will raise the siege of Orléans.

TO D'ALENÇON

You are very welcome. The more there are gathered together of the blood of the King of France, the better it will be.

Chinon, Poitiers, Tours, and Blois

March–April, 1429

FOR THREE WEEKS I was examined by learned men in Chinon and Poitiers, and the King received a sign concerning what I had done before he would believe in me.

And the scholars were of this opinion, that they could see nothing but good in my undertaking.

HER WORDS TO HER ESCORT

I know that I shall have much to do in Poitiers. But my Lord will help me. In God's name, let us go on!

HER ANSWERS TO HER EXAMINERS

I do not know A from B.

I am come from the King of Heaven to raise the siege of Orléans and to lead the Dauphin to Reims to be crowned and anointed.

In God's name, I did not come to Poitiers to give signs! Take me to Orléans, and I will show you a sign and for what I am sent!

The voice has told me that it is God's will to deliver the people of France from the calamity that is upon them.

(*Guillaume Aimery answers, "If it be God's will to deliver them, then there is no need for soldiers." Then Jehanne:*)

In God's name! The soldiers will fight, and God will give the victory!

Has one of you paper and ink? Then write what I tell you: "You, Suffolk, Glasdale, and La Pole, in the name of the King of Heaven I summon you to depart into England."

✝

I was ill content with so much questioning, being held back from accomplishing that for which I was sent. The time was ripe to act.

I asked my Lord's messengers what I should do. And they answered me, saying, "Take up the banner of your Lord." And thereupon I had a banner made.

The field of it was sown with lilies, and therein was our Lord holding the world, with two angels, one on either hand. It was white, and on it there were written the names *Jhesus Maria*, and it was fringed with silk.

I had the sword which I had brought from Vaucouleurs.

I sent to make search for another sword in the church of Saint Catherine at Fierbois, behind the altar. It was found there presently, all rusted, and on it there were five crosses. And the priests there rubbed it, and the rust fell away of itself.

I loved that sword, because it was found in the church of Saint Catherine, whom I loved.

But I loved my banner forty times better than my sword. And when I went against the enemy, I carried my banner myself, lest I kill any. I have never killed a man.

I knew that I would surely raise the siege of Orléans, for it had been revealed to me. And this I had told my King.

HER WORDS TO CHARLES

I shall last a year, and but little longer: we must think to do good work in that year. Four things are laid upon me: to drive out the English; to bring you to be crowned and anointed at Reims; to rescue the Duke of Orléans from the hands of the English; and to raise the siege of Orléans.

✝

And the King set to work, giving me ten or twelve thousand men, and I went to Orléans.

Letter, March 22, 1429

+   JHESUS MARIA   +

King of England, and you, Duke of Bedford, who call yourself Regent of the Kingdom of France; you, William de la Pole, Earl of Suffolk; John, Lord Talbot; and you, Thomas, Lord Scales, who call yourselves lieutenants of the said Duke of Bedford: Do justice to the King of Heaven; surrender to the Maid, who is sent here from God, King of Heaven, the keys of all the good towns you have taken and violated in France. She is come from God to uphold the blood royal. She is ready to make peace if you will do justice, relinquishing France and paying for what you have withheld.

As to you, you archers and men-at-arms, gentle and others, who are before the town of Orléans, go hence into your own country in God's name; and if you do not so, expect to hear news of the Maid, who will shortly come to see you, to your very great damage.

King of England, if you do not so, I am a commander, and in whatever place in France I come upon your men, I will make them leave it, will they or nill they; and if they will not yield obedience, I will have them all slain. I am sent here from God, King of Heaven, to put you, hand to hand, out of all France. Yet if they will yield obedience, I will grant them mercy.

And think not otherwise: for you shall not hold the Kingdom of France from God, King of Heaven, Saint Mary's son, but King Charles shall hold it, the true heir. For so God, King of Heaven, wills it; and so it has been revealed to him by the Maid, and he shall enter Paris with a fair company.

If you will not believe this news from God and the Maid, wherever we find you, there we shall strike; and we shall raise such a battle-cry as there has not been in France in a thousand years, if you will not do justice. And know surely that the King of Heaven will send more strength to the Maid than you can bring against her and her good soldiers in any assault. And when the blows begin, it shall be seen whose right is the better before the God of Heaven.

You, Duke of Bedford: The Maid prays and beseeches you not to bring on your own destruction. If you will do her justice, you may yet come in her company there where the French shall do the fairest deed that ever was done for Christendom. So answer if you will make peace in the city of Orléans. And if you do not so, consider your great danger speedily.

Written this Tuesday in Holy Week.

Delivery of Orléans

April–May, 1429

March from Blois to Orléans, April 28–29

Trust in God. Make confession, and be shriven, for so God will help you. Being shriven, you shall have the victory, by God's help.

TO DUNOIS, COMING OUT
FROM ORLÉANS TO MEET HER

Are you the Bastard of Orléans?

Was it you who counselled that we should come here on this side of the river, and not go straight to where Talbot and the English are?

(*He answers, "Yes, I, and others wiser than I, believing it safer and surer." Then Jehanne:*)

In God's name! our Lord God's counsel is surer and wiser than yours. You thought to deceive me; it is yourself that you deceive. For I bring you better succour than ever came to captain or town, which is succour from the King of Heaven. Nor is it granted for love of me; but God, at the prayer of Saint Louis and Saint

Charlemagne, has taken pity on the town of Orléans, nor will he suffer the enemy to hold both the Duke of Orléans' person and his town.

Entry into Orléans, April 29

TO THE PEOPLE

My Lord has sent me to succour this good town of Orléans.

Hope in God. If you have good hope and faith in him, you shall be delivered from your enemies.

Orléans: Capture of the
English Fortress of Saint-Loup, May 4

TO HER PAGE

Ha! wretched boy! you did not tell me that French blood was flowing!
Where are those who should arm me?
To horse! To horse!

Evening of the Same Day, Ascension Eve

TO HER CHAPLAIN

Tomorrow I will not go out to fight nor put on armor, in reverence to the feast day, I will make my confession and receive the sacrament.

Let none tomorrow dare to leave the town and go out to fight, unless he has first gone to confession. And let them beware lest women of evil fame follow them: because, for sin, God will permit the loss of this war.

Letter, May 5
(Fastened to an arrow and shot into the English lines)

You Englishmen, who have no right in this Kingdom of France, the King of Heaven sends you word and warning, by me Jehanne the Maid, to abandon your forts and depart into your own country, or I will raise such a war-cry against you as shall be remembered forever. And this I write to you for the third and last time, nor shall I write further.

I should send you my letter more decently, but you detain my heralds. For you have kept my herald Guyenne. Send him to me, and I will send you some of your men who were taken at Saint-Loup, for not all were killed.

Orléans: Capture of the
English Fortress of the Augustines, May 6

TO HER SOLDIERS

In God's name! let us go on bravely!

Evening of the Same Day: Council of War

TO ONE OF THE CAPTAINS

You have been with your council and I have been with mine. Believe me that the counsel of my Lord will be accomplished and will stand, and this counsel of yours will perish.

THEN TO HER CHAPLAIN

Tomorrow, rise very early, earlier than you did today, and do the best that you can. Keep close to me all day, for tomorrow I shall have much to do and greater things than I have had to do yet. And tomorrow blood will flow from my body, above my breast.

Orléans: Capture of the Bridge, May 7

I was the first to set a ladder against the fortress on the bridge, and, as I raised it, I was wounded in the throat by a cross-bow bolt. But Saint Catherine comforted me greatly. And I did not cease to ride and do my work.

TO HER SOLDIERS

Courage! Do not fall back: in a little the place will be yours. Watch! when you see the wind blow my banner against the bulwark, you shall take it!

In, in, the place is yours!

TO THE ENGLISH CAPTAIN

Glasdale, Glasdale, yield, yield to the King of Heaven. You have called me "whore": I pity your soul and the souls of your men.

TO THOSE WHO OFFERED
TO CHARM HER WOUND

I would rather die than do what I know to be sin.

Orléans: The English Raise the Siege, May 8

TO HER SOLDIERS

In God's name! they go. Let them depart. And go we to give thanks to God. We shall not follow them farther, for it is Sunday. Seek not to harm them. It suffices me that they go.

Return to Court

May–June, 1429

In Council

TO CHARLES

NOBLE DAUPHIN, hold no more so many and such long councils, but come as quickly as you can to Reims to take the crown.

Whenever I am unhappy, because men will not believe me in the things that I say at God's bidding, I go apart and pray to God, complaining to him that those to whom I speak do not easily believe me. And when I have made my prayer to God, I hear a voice that says to me: "Child of God, go, go, go! I shall be with you to help you. Go!" And when I hear that voice I feel a great joy. Indeed, I would that I might ever be in that state.

TO JEAN D'AULON

My counsellors are three. There is one who remains with me always, another comes and goes and visits me often, and the third is he with whom the other two take counsel.

The Loire Campaign

June, 1429

Capture of Jargeau, June 11–12

THE LEADERS OF OUR PARTY answered the English that they could not have the two weeks' delay for which they had asked, but that they must leave, they and their horses, that very hour. As for me, I said, "Let the garrison in Jargeau go in their small-clothes with their lives safe, if they will. Otherwise they will be taken by assault."

TO THE FRENCH CAPTAINS

Fear not, however many they be! Neither weigh difficulties. God guides our work. Were I not certain that God guides this work, I would rather keep sheep than expose myself to such perils.

TO D'ALENÇON

Fear not. The hour is ripe when God pleases. We must work when God wills. "Toil and God will toil."

Ah, noble Duke, are you afraid? Do you not know that I have promised your wife to bring you back safe and sound?

On, noble Duke, to the assault!

TO HER SOLDIERS

Friends, friends, on, on! Our Lord has condemned the English. This very hour they are ours. Be of good heart!

Battle of Patay, June 18

TO THE CAPTAINS

In God's name! we must fight them. Did they hang from clouds we should have them! For God is sending them to us for us to punish. And today our noble King shall have the greatest victory he has won in many days. My council has told me that they are all ours.

Ride bravely, and we shall have good leading!

Orléans, June 24

TO THE CAPTAINS

Sound trumpets and to horse!

It is time to rejoin our noble King Charles and set him on the road to his anointing at Reims.

Letter, June 25

To the loyal Frenchmen of Tournai

+   JHESUS MARIA   +

Noble loyal Frenchmen of Tournai town, the Maid
sends you news from these parts: that in one week she
has chased the English out of all the places that they
held along the River Loire, either by assault or otherwise, in which encounters many English were killed
and captured, and she has routed them in a pitched battle. Know too that the Earl of Suffolk, his brother La
Pole, Lord Talbot, Lord Scales, with Sir John Fastolf
and many other knights and captains have been captured, and a brother of the Earl of Suffolk's and Glasdale were killed.

Keep yourselves loyal Frenchmen, I pray you. I pray
you too and beg you to be ready, all of you, to come to
the anointing of noble King Charles at Reims, where
we shall shortly be. And come out to meet us when you
hear that we are near. I commend you to God. God
keep you and give you grace to maintain the good cause
of the Kingdom of France.

Written at Gien, the xxvth day of June.

The March to Reims

June–July, 1429

Gien, June 25–27

WE MUST GO TO REIMS. When once the King is crowned and anointed, his enemies' strength will steadily grow less, and finally they will have no power to harm him or the Kingdom.

TO THOSE WHO SPOKE OF
THE DANGERS OF THE WAY

All this I know well, but I account it as nothing. By my staff! I shall lead noble King Charles and his company safely, and he shall be anointed in Reims!

TO CHARLES AND THE CAPTAINS

Go bravely: all will be well. Have no fear. We shall find none who can harm us; indeed, we shall meet with no resistance. I have no fear for lack of men. There will be many to follow me.

Letter, July 4

To the nobles and burgesses of Troyes

+   JHESUS MARIA   +

Very dear and good friends (if you do not prevent it), nobles, burgesses, and townsmen of the town of Troyes: Jehanne the Maid, on behalf of the King of Heaven, her rightful and sovereign Lord, in whose royal service she daily goes, sends this and bids you render true obedience and fealty to the noble King of France, who will very shortly be at Reims and Paris, whoever may come against him, and in his good towns of this holy Kingdom, by the help of King Jesus.

Loyal Frenchmen, come out to meet King Charles and let there be no defaulting. Nor if you do this, fear for your bodies or your goods. And, if you do not, I promise and declare to you, upon your lives, that by God's help we shall enter into all the towns which should be of his holy Kingdom, and there make good and firm peace, whoever may come against us.

To God I commend you. God keep you if it be his pleasure. Make answer shortly.

Before the town of Troyes, written at Saint-Phal,
Tuesday the fourth day of July.

Siege of Troyes, July 5–11

The people of Troyes, I think, sent Friar Richard out to me, saying that they doubted whether I was sent by God. And when he came out, he came towards me making the sign of the cross and sprinkling holy-water. And I said to him, "Come on bravely, I shall not fly away."

TO CHARLES

Noble Dauphin, bid your men go and lay siege to Troyes, neither draw out further these overlong councils. In God's name! within three days, I shall bring you into the town, either by friendship or by force. And false Burgundy will be much astonished.

HER SUMMONS

Yield you to the King of Heaven and to noble King Charles!

Châlons, July 14–15

TO GÉRARDIN D'ÉPINAL, OF DOMREMY

I fear nothing but treachery.

TO CHARLES

Go forward bravely. Fear nothing. If you will go forward like a man, you shall have your whole Kingdom!

Letter, July 17

To the Duke of Burgundy

+ JHESUS MARIA +

High and redoubted prince, Duke of Burgundy: Jehanne the Maid begs you on behalf of the King of Heaven, my rightful and sovereign Lord, that the King of France and you make a good and firm peace which shall long endure. Forgive each other heartily and wholly, as loyal Christians should do; and, if it is your pleasure to make war, then go against the Saracens. Prince of Burgundy, I pray and beseech and beg you, as humbly as I can beg, to make war no longer in the holy Kingdom of France, and now and at once to order away your men who are in any places or fortresses of the said holy Kingdom. And for his part, the noble King of France is ready to make peace with you, saving his honor, if you do not prevent it.

And I give you to know on behalf of the King of Heaven, my rightful and sovereign Lord, for your good

and honor and upon your life, that you will win no battle in France against loyal Frenchmen, and that all
those who make war in the said holy Kingdom of
France make war against King Jesus, King of Heaven
and all the world, my rightful and sovereign Lord.

And, hands clasped, I pray you and beg you not to do
battle nor make war against us—neither you, your soldiers, nor your subjects. And know surely that, whatever number of soldiers you bring against us, they will
win nothing from us; and a pitiful thing will be that
great battle and the blood that will be shed therein by
those who come there against us.

It is three weeks now since I wrote to you and sent
you a fair letter by a herald, that you should come to the
King's anointing, which is this day, Sunday, xviith day
of this present month of July, being performed in the
town of Reims: to which I have had no answer, nor
heard any news since of the said herald.

To God I commend you, may he keep you if it be his
pleasure. And I pray God to send us a good peace.

Written in the said place of Reims,
the said xviith day of July.

Reims: The Coronation

July 17, 1429

As far as I know, my King willingly accepted the crown which he found at Reims. He did this to hasten his undertaking and because the townsmen asked it, wishing to be relieved of the burden of his soldiers. If he had waited he would have had a crown a thousand times richer.

My banner was in the church at Reims when the King was anointed. I held it myself for a little. It had shared in the toil; it was just that it should share in the honor.

TO ONE WHO PRAISED HER

saying,
"Such deeds as you have done were never seen,
their like is not to be read in any book"

My Lord has a book in which no scholar has read, how perfect soever he be in scholarship.

From Reims to Paris

July–August–September, 1429

To loyal Frenchmen dwelling in the town of Reims

My DEAR AND GOOD FRIENDS, the good and loyal Frenchmen of the town of Reims: Jehanne the Maid sends you her news and prays and begs you to have no fear for the good cause which she is leading for the blood royal. And I promise and declare to you that I will not abandon you as long as I shall live.

It is true that the King has made a truce with the Duke of Burgundy for two weeks, in accordance with which he is to surrender the town of Paris peaceably to him at the end of two weeks (only do not be at all surprised if I do not enter there so soon); however, I am not satisfied with this manner of truce, and I do not know if I will keep it, but if I do keep it, it will be only to preserve the King's honor; however, in any case, they will not again abuse the blood royal, for I shall keep and hold the King's army together, so as to be all ready at the end of the said two weeks if they do not make peace.

Therefore, my very dear and perfect friends, I pray you not to be uneasy as long as I shall live; only I beg you to keep a good watch and to guard the King's good town, and let me know if there are any traitors who would harm you, and, as shortly as I can, I will put a stop to them. Send me also your news.

To God I commend you, may he keep you.

Written this Friday, vth day of August, near Provins,
at a camp in the fields on the road to Paris.

Near Crépy-en-Valois, August 10 or 11

TO THE ARCHBISHOP OF REIMS

This is a good people. I have seen no other people so joyful at the coming of our most noble King. And would that I might be so happy, when I shall end my days, as to be buried in the earth of this place!

(*He answers, "O Jehanne, where do you expect to die?" Then Jehanne:*)

Wherever it may please God, for I am no more sure of the hour or the season or the place than you. And would that it were pleasing to God my maker that I might now turn back, laying off my arms, and go to serve my father and my mother, keeping their sheep with my sister and my brothers; they would be very glad to see me!

Compiègne, August 23

TO D'ALENÇON

Good Duke, get your men ready, and the other captains' men too. By my staff! I want a nearer sight of Paris than I have had yet!

Attack on Paris
Retreat to Saint-Denis
Departure from Saint-Denis

September 8–13, 1429

THE COMMANDERS WANTED to skirmish before Paris. But I meant to go farther and to cross the moats.

I gave the orders for a skirmish before Paris. I was wounded in the moat.

By my staff! the place would have been taken!

✚

The voice told me to stay in Saint-Denis. But the captains took me away against my will. Had I not been wounded I would not have gone. In five days I was well again.

I made an offering of a sword and armor in Saint-Denis—a whole suit of my white armor and a sword which I had won before Paris. That is the custom among soldiers when they are wounded. And because I had been wounded before Paris, I offered them to Saint Denis, for his name is the war-cry of France.

In Saint-Denis I stood sponsor for two children. I liked to name boys *Charles*, in honor of my King, and girls *Jehanne*.

From Saint-Denis to Compiègne

September, 1429–May, 1430

Bourges, October, 1429

TO HER HOSTESS

I AM SENT to comfort the poor and needy.

WHEN WOMEN BROUGHT ROSARIES
FOR HER TO TOUCH

You touch them: they will be as much bettered by your touch as by mine!

Capture of Saint-Pierre-le-Moustier, November, 1429

TO HER SOLDIERS

All fall to with faggots and hurdles! We must make a bridge!

Letter, November 9, 1429

To my dear and good friends the churchmen, burgesses, and townsmen of the town of Riom.

Dear and good friends, you already know how the town of Saint-Pierre-le-Moustier was taken by assault.

And with God's help I intend to clear out the other places which are against the King. But because great quantities of powder, arrows, and other furnishings of war were expended before the said town and because the lords who are in this town and I are poorly provided therewith to go to besiege La Charité, whither we are going speedily, I pray you, as you love the King's good and honor and those of all others here, instantly to send help for the said siege, of powder, saltpeter, sulphur, arrows, heavy arbalests, and other furnishings of war. And deal herein in such fashion that, for lack of the said powder and other furnishings of war, the matter will not be prolonged, nor you be said to be herein neglectful or unconsenting.

Dear and good friends, our Lord keep you.

Written at Moulins, the ninth day of November.

Jehanne

Montfaucon or Jargeau, November, 1429

I knew Catherine de la Rochelle at Jargeau and at Montfaucon-en-Berry.

She told me that a white lady dressed in cloth-of-gold came to her and told her to go through the loyal towns, and that the King should give her heralds and trumpeters to cry that whoever had gold, silver, or hidden treasure must straightway bring it. And any who did not, and who had treasure hidden, she would recognize and would know how to find their treasure. And this was to pay my soldiers. And I told her to go back to her husband, and do her housework and bring up her children. And, to be certain, I spoke to Saint Margaret or Saint Catherine, who told me that this Catherine's undertaking was all foolishness and naught. I wrote to my King that I would tell him what to do in the matter. And when I saw him I told him that this Catherine's undertaking was all foolishness and naught. But Friar Richard wanted to have her put to work. And he and Catherine were much displeased with me.

I asked Catherine if her white lady came every night, and, if it were so, I would spend a night with her. And I went to bed with her and stayed awake until midnight and saw nothing, and then I fell asleep. In the morning I asked if she had come, and Catherine said that she had, but that I was asleep and she had not been able to wake me. Then I asked her if she would come again the day after, and Catherine said yes. So I slept that day, so that I could keep awake at night. And the next night I went to bed with Catherine, and watched all night. But I saw nothing, though I kept asking if she would not come. And Catherine always answered, "Yes, soon."

When she wanted to go to the Duke of Burgundy to make peace, I told her that I did not think that peace was to be got from him except at the point of a lance.

Catherine did not advise me to go to La Charité. She said it was too cold and that she was not going.

Defeat at La Charité, November, 1429

I wanted to go into France, but the captains said that it would be better first to go before La Charité.

Letter, March 16, 1430

To my very dear and good friends, the churchmen, burgesses, and other townsmen of the town of Reims.

Very dear and well beloved, whom I much long to see, I, Jehanne the Maid, have received your letter making mention that you fear you will be besieged. Please know that you will not be, if I can meet with them very shortly. And if it should happen that I do not meet with them and they should come before you, then shut your gates, for I shall very shortly be in your neighborhood. And if they are there I shall make them put on their spurs in such haste that they will not know where to find them, and raise the siege, if it is begun, so shortly that it will be very soon.

I write no more now, except: be you ever good and loyal. I pray God to have you in his keeping.

Written at Sully, the xvith day of March.

I would send you some further news, with which you would be most joyful, but I fear this letter may be taken on the road and the said news be seen.

Jehanne

Letter, March 28

To my very dear and good friends, the churchmen, aldermen, burgesses, and townsmen of the good town of Reims.

Very dear and good friends, may it please you to know that I have received your letter making mention of how it was reported to the King that there were many evil-doers in the good town of Reims. Please know likewise that it is very true that it was indeed reported to him, as well as that there were many of them who had made a compact and were to betray the town and let the Burgundians in. And, since then, the King has learned the contrary, because you have sent him the truth of the matter, wherefore he is greatly pleased with you, and you may believe that you are surely in his good grace and if you were pressed he would succour you, as far as the siege is concerned. And he knows well that you have much to bear from the hardships that our traitorous Burgundian enemies cause you, and he will deliver you from them, if God please, very shortly, that is, as soon as ever it can be done. So I pray and beg you, very dear friends, to hold the said good town safely for the King, and to keep very good watch.

You shall soon hear good news from me more at large. At present I write you no more, save that all Brittany is French and the Duke is to send the King three thousand soldiers paid for two months.

To God I commend you, may he keep you.

Written at Sully, the xxviiith of March.

Jehanne

Melun, Week of April 16

Last Easter week,—I was standing near the moat at Melun,—my voices told me that I would be taken prisoner before Saint John's Day, and that it must be so, and that I must not be frightened but accept it willingly, and God would help me.

And I begged of my voices that, when I should be taken, I might die straightway, without long travail in prison.

After it was revealed to me at Melun that I would be taken prisoner, I most often referred the conduct of the war to the will of the captains. But I did not tell them that it had been revealed to me that I would be taken.

Lagny, April or May

I was told that the girls of the town were gathered before the statue of Our Lady, and wanted me to come and pray God and Our Lady to bring a baby to life. And I went and prayed with the others. And finally life appeared in him and he yawned three times. Then he was baptized, and soon after he died and was buried in consecrated ground. For three days, so they said, he had shown no sign of life, and he was as black as my jacket.

But when he yawned his color began to come back. And I was on my knees with the other girls before Our Lady, praying.

Crépy-en-Valois, May 22

TO HER SOLDIERS

By my staff, we are enough! I shall go to see my good friends in Compiègne.

Capture

May, 1430

Compiègne, May 23

I CAME TO COMPIÈGNE at a secret hour in the morning, and entered the town, I think, without our enemies knowing it. And the same day, towards evening, I made the sally in which I was taken.

I had a sword which had been taken from a Burgundian. I got it at Lagny, and I carried it from Lagny to Compiègne because it was a good war-sword, good to give good buffets and good thrusts. I was riding a half-courser.

I did not know that I would be taken that day.

I crossed the bridge and the bulwark, and went with a company of our soldiers against Monseigneur de Luxembourg's men. I drove them back twice, as far as the Burgundian camp, and a third time half-way. Then the English who were there cut us off, both me and my men, coming between me and the bulwark. And so my men fell back. And as I fell back flankwise into the fields towards Picardie, near the bulwark, I was taken.

Captivity

Beaulieu, Beaurevoir, Arras, Le Crotoy, Rouen

May, 1430–February, 1431

Beaulieu

Wherever I have been a prisoner I have wanted to escape. When I was in the castle of Beaulieu I would have shut up my guards in the tower, had not the porter seen me and come to me.

TO JEAN D'AULON

The places that the King of Heaven has reduced to obedience and restored to the hands of noble King Charles through me shall none of them be won back by his enemies, so long as he is diligent in guarding them.

Beaurevoir

I was in the tower of Beaurevoir about four months.

The reason why I jumped from the tower was that I had heard that all the people in Compiègne, even to children of seven years, were to be put to fire and sword. And I would rather be dead than live on after such a destruction of good people. That was one reason. The other was that I knew that I was sold to the English, and

I thought death would be better than to be in their hands who were my enemies. Almost every day Saint Catherine told me that I must not jump, that God would help me and the people of Compiègne too. And I said to Saint Catherine that if God meant to help the people of Compiègne, I wanted to be there.

When I knew that the English were coming, I was greatly troubled. Yet still, and many times, my voices forbade me to jump. And at last, for fear of the English, I did jump, commending myself to God and Our Lady, and I was hurt. And after I had jumped, Saint Catherine's voice told me to be of good cheer and that I would be healed and the people of Compiègne would have succour.

I did it, not in despair, but in hope to save my life and to go to the succour of many good people in distress. And afterwards I confessed it, and begged our Lord to forgive me for it, and I have our Lord's pardon for it. And I think it was not right for me to jump—it was wrong.

✝

Mademoiselle de Luxembourg and Madame de Beau-revoir offered me woman's clothing or cloth to make it, and asked me to wear it. I answered that I had not our Lord's permission, and that it was not yet time.

If I might have done it, I would sooner have done it at the asking of those two ladies than of any other ladies in France, except my Queen.

Mademoiselle de Luxembourg asked Monseigneur de Luxembourg not to let me be given up to the English.

Arras

In Arras I saw a painting in the hands of a Scot, and in it there was a likeness of me fully armed, presenting a letter to my King and kneeling on one knee.

Rouen

TO JEAN DE LUXEMBOURG

I know well that these English will do me to death, thinking that after I am dead they will win the Kingdom of France. But if the Goddamns were a hundred thousand more than they are now, they shall not have the Kingdom.

She is Cited to Appear for Trial,
February 20, 1431

TO THE BEARER OF THE BISHOP'S ORDER

I ask him to summon the churchmen who will take part with him in this matter from French territory as well as from English. Further, I humbly pray him to let me hear mass tomorrow before I appear before them. Tell him that.

The Trial

February–May, 1431

CONCERNING MY FATHER and mother and what I have done since I took the road to France I will willingly swear to tell the truth. But the revelations which have come to me from God I have never told or revealed to anyone, except to Charles, my King. Nor would I reveal them if I were to be beheaded. A week from today I shall have learned whether I may reveal them.

I will not say the "Our Father" for you unless you will hear me in confession.

I do not accept your prohibition. And if I escape from prison, no one can accuse me of breaking my faith, for I have pledged it to no one.

I protest against being kept in chains and irons.

It is true that I have wished, and that I still wish, what is permissible for any captive: to escape!

Sessions in a Room off the Hall of State, Rouen Castle

I

THURSDAY, FEBRUARY 22

I took your oath yesterday. That should suffice you. You burden me too greatly.

If you were rightly informed concerning me, you should wish that I were out of your hands. I have done nothing but by revelation.

If now I were in a wood I should hear the voices coming to me.

At this time you shall not get from me the shape in which the voice appeared.

There is no day that I do not hear the voice. And indeed I need it. I have never asked it for any other reward than, in the end, the salvation of my soul.

II

SATURDAY, FEBRUARY 24

Give me leave to speak! Upon my faith, you may ask me things that I will not tell you. It is possible that concerning many things that you may ask me I would not answer the truth—things that concern my revelations. For perhaps you might force me to tell something that I have sworn not to tell, and so perjure myself—which you ought not to wish. And I tell you this: Consider well your saying that you are my judge, for you are assuming a great burden, and you burden me too greatly.

I come, sent by God. I have no business here. I pray you, send me back to God from whom I am come.

When did you last hear the voice?
I heard it yesterday and today. Yesterday I heard it three times—once in the morning, once at vespers, and the third time when the bells were ringing for "Hail Mary" in the evening.

I was sleeping and the voice waked me. And I thanked it, sitting up in my bed, and joining my hands.

I prayed it to counsel me in what I should answer, telling it to ask counsel of our Lord in that. And the voice told me that I should answer bravely and that God would help me.

You say that you are my judge. Take thought over what you are doing. For, truly, I am sent from God, and you are putting yourself in great danger.

I firmly believe, as firmly as I believe the Christian faith and that God has redeemed us from the pains of Hell, that the voice comes from God and at his bidding.

I am more afraid of doing wrong by saying what would displease those voices than I am to answer you. And as to these questions, I ask you to grant me time.

Do you think it displeasing to God to have the truth told?
My voices have told me to tell certain things to the King, not to you! Last night they told me many things for my King's good, and I would willingly drink no wine until Easter to have him know them now. He would sit down to his dinner with a lighter heart.

Can you not persuade the voice to do your will
and take a message to your King?
I do not know if the voice would obey me, unless it were God's will and God permitted it.
   But for God's grace, I could do nothing.

Has your council told you that you will escape from prison?
Am I supposed to tell you that?

Do you know that you are in God's grace?
If I am not, God put me there, and if I am, God keep me
there! I should be the saddest creature in all the world if
I knew I were not in God's grace. I think, if I were in sin,
that the voice would not come to me. And I wish that
everyone heard it as I do!

Did the voice, in your girlhood,
tell you to hate the Burgundians?
After I understood that the voices were for the King of
France, I did not like the Burgundians. And the Burgundians will have war, unless they do as they ought. I
know that from the voice.

Did you, in your girlhood, have a strong inclination
to harm the Burgundians?
I had a strong desire for my King to have his Kingdom.

Should you like to be given a woman's dress?
Give me one: I will take it and go! Otherwise I will not
take it. I am content with this attire, since it pleases
God that I should wear it.

III

How have you fared since Saturday?
You can see very well how I have fared. I have fared as well as I could.

Have you heard the voice that comes to you, since Saturday?
Yes indeed. I have heard it many times.

Did you hear it in this room on Saturday?
That has nothing to do with your trial! I did hear it here.

I did not understand it well. I did not understand anything that I could repeat to you until I had returned to my room.

It told me to answer you bravely.

I asked the voice for counsel on the things about which I was questioned.

In some points I have had counsel. Concerning others that I may be asked to answer I will not answer without leave. If I were to answer without leave, perhaps I should not have the voices for protection. But when I shall have leave from our Lord I shall not be afraid to speak, for then I shall have good protection.

The voice is Saint Catherine's voice and Saint Margaret's. And their heads are crowned with a fair crown, most richly and most preciously. Concerning that, I have leave from our Lord. And if you doubt it, send to Poitiers where I was questioned before.

I know very well that it is they, and I can very well tell them apart!

Which of them appeared to you first?
I did not recognize them as soon as that. I knew once, but I have forgotten. If I can have leave, I will tell you willingly; it is set down in the register at Poitiers. And I had comfort from Saint Michael.

Is it long since you first had the voice of Saint Michael?
I am not saying "the voice of Saint Michael"; I am telling you of great comfort.

I have told you often enough that they are Saint Catherine and Saint Margaret. Believe me if you like!

Are you forbidden to tell what sign you have
that they are Saint Catherine and Saint Margaret?
I have not yet clearly understood whether that is forbidden me or not.

Did God command you to put on men's clothing?
My clothing is a small matter, one of the least. But I did not put on men's clothing by the counsel of any man on earth. I did not put on this clothing, nor do anything else, except at the bidding of God and the angels.

All that I have done is by our Lord's bidding. And if he had bid me put on other clothing I should have put it on because it was at his bidding.

All that I have done at our Lord's bidding I believe that I have done rightly. And I expect good protection for it and good succour.

When you saw the voice coming to you, was there any light?
There was light all about, and so there should be! All light does not come to you.

Was there an angel over your King's head when you saw him for the first time?
By Blessed Mary! If there was, I know nothing about it. I did not see one.

Was there any light?
There were more than three hundred knights and fifty torches—without counting the spiritual light!

How did it happen that your King
had faith in what you said?
He had good tokens; and because of his learned men.

What revelations did your King have?
You shall not get that from me yet, nor this year!

Did you ever offer prayers to the end
that your sword should be more fortunate?
It is a good thing to know that I would want my arms
to be fortunate.

IV

THURSDAY, MARCH 1

About what I know which concerns this trial I will
freely tell the truth, and I will tell you just as much as I
should tell if I were before the Pope of Rome.

What have you to say as to our lord the Pope,
and as to whom you believe is the true Pope?
Are there two?

Her letter beginning "King of England"
having been read to her, she is asked:

Do you recognize this letter?
Yes, except for three words—that is, first, where it says, "surrender to the Maid," there should be "surrender to the King." Then where it says "a commander," and, thirdly, where there is "hand to hand," those words were not in the letter that I sent. And no lord spoke that letter, but I myself spoke it before it was sent, although it was shown to some of my party. And before seven years are done the English will have left behind a greater stake than they did before Orléans; they shall lose everything in France. And the English will have a greater loss than they have ever had in France. And that will be through a great victory which God will send the French.

How do you know this?
I know it through a revelation which was made to me. And it will happen in less than seven years. I should be very sorry if it were to be delayed that long. I know it by revelation as well as I know that you are before me now.

When will this happen?
I know neither the day nor the hour.

In what year will it happen?
You shall not get that yet. But I wish it were to be before
Saint John's Day!

*Have you talked with Saint Catherine
and Saint Margaret since Tuesday?*
Yes, but I do not know the hour.

What day was it?
Yesterday and today. There is no day that I do not hear
them.

Do you always see them in the same dress?
I always see them in the same form. I know nothing of
their garments.

What form do you see?
I see the face.

Have the saints who appear to you hair?
It is a good thing to know!

Was their hair long and hanging?
I do not know. And I do not know if there was any semblance of arms or of other members. They spoke well and fairly, and I understood them well.

How do they speak if they do not have members?
I leave that to God. They speak the French tongue.

Does not Saint Margaret speak English?
Why should she speak English when she is not of the English party?

Have the voices told you that you will be freed from prison within three months?
That does not concern your trial. However, I do not know when I shall be freed. Those who would put me out of this world may well be leaving it before me.

Has your council told you that you will be freed from your present prison?
Talk to me in three months; I will answer you on it. Ask those who are present here, upon their oaths, if that concerns this trial.

They agree that it does.
I have always told you that you shall not know all. I must needs be freed one day. But I want leave, if I am to tell you. Therefore I ask for time.

Have the voices forbidden you to tell the truth?
Do you want me to tell you what concerns the King of France? There are many things which do not concern this trial. And I know well that my King will win the Kingdom of France—I know it as well as I know that you are before me to judge me. I should be dead, were it not for the revelation that comforts me each day.

In what form was Saint Michael when he appeared to you?
I saw no crown upon him. I know nothing of his garments.

Was he naked?
Do you think that God has not wherewith to clothe him?

Had he hair?
Why should it have been cut off? I have not seen Blessed Michael since I left the castle of Crotoy; I do not see him very often.

Had he his scales?
I do not know. I feel great joy when I see him; I think
that, when I see him, I am not in mortal sin.

When you confess, do you believe that you are in mortal sin?
I do not know if I have been in mortal sin: I do not believe that I have done the works thereof. Please God I
have not been! Please God I shall not do, and that I have
not done, things by which my soul will be burdened!

What sign did you give to your King
that you came from God?
I have always answered you that you shall not draw
that from my lips. Go and ask him!

Do you not know the sign that you gave to your King?
You shall not learn that from me.

It concerns this trial.
As to what I have promised to keep secret, that I will
not tell you. I promised in such a place that I cannot tell
you without perjury.

V

SATURDAY, MARCH 3

*You have said that Saint Michael has wings. But you have
not spoken about the bodies or limbs of Saint Catherine and
Saint Margaret. What have you to say about those?*
I have told you what I know, and I will not answer anything more. I have seen Saint Michael and Saint Catherine and Saint Margaret well enough to know that
they are saints in Paradise.

*Do you know by revelation that you will escape
from prison?*
That does not concern your trial! Would you have me
speak against myself?

Have your voices told you something about it?
Yes indeed! They have told me that I shall be freed. But
I know neither the day nor the hour. And they have told
me to be of good cheer, bravely!

*Do you believe that you would have failed in your duty or
committed a mortal sin if you had put on women's clothing?*
I do best by obeying and serving my sovereign Lord—
that is, God.

Did you ever say that pennons made
after the fashion of your own were lucky?
I sometimes said to my men, "Go in bravely among the English," and went in myself.

Did you tell them to carry their pennons bravely
and they would have good luck?
I told them things that have happened, and things that shall happen yet.

Do you know whether people of your faction ever had
services or masses or prayers offered for you?
I do not know. And if they had services offered for me, they did not do it at my bidding. And if they prayed for me, I think they did nothing wrong.

Do those of your faction truly believe
that you are sent from God?
I do not know if they believe it; I leave that to their hearts. But if they do not believe it, even so I am sent from God!

Do you think that if they believe you are sent
from God they believe rightly?
If they believe that I am sent from God, they are not deceived.

Did you not know what was in their hearts
when they kissed your feet and
your hands and your garments?

There were many who wanted to see me, but they kissed my garments only when I could not help it. But the poor wanted to come to me because I did them no hurt—rather, I supported them to the best of my power.

Why did you not enter La Charité,
since you were commanded to by God?

Who told you that I was commanded to enter it?

Sessions in Her Prison

I

SATURDAY, MARCH 10

I promise to tell you the truth of what concerns your trial. And the more you make me swear, the longer it will be before I tell you.

If your voices had told you to make a sally
and given you to understand that
you would be captured, would you have gone?
Had I known the hour and that I would be taken, I
should not have wanted to go. But I would have done
their bidding in the end, no matter what was to be-
fall me.

What is the sign that came to your King?
It is beautiful and honored and to be believed, and it is
good and the most precious on earth.

Why do you not want to tell your sign, or show it, just as you
wanted Catherine de la Rochelle to show hers?
If Catherine's sign had been shown before notable
churchmen and others—archbishops and bishops,
such as the archbishop of Reims and other bishops
whose names I do not know—as the sign of which I
speak was shown (and Charles de Bourbon was present
also, and Monseigneur de la Trémoïlle and the Duke of
Alençon and many other knights, who saw it and heard
it as well as I see you who are questioning me), then I
should not have asked to know her sign.

Does the sign still exist?
It is a good thing to know, and that it will exist for a
thousand years, and more! *Love*

I will not tell you anything more: no one could describe so precious a thing as that sign. However, the
sign that you need to have is for God to deliver me out
of your hands. That is the surest sign that he could send
you!

*When the sign came to your King, what reverence
did you show it? Did it come from God?*
I thanked our Lord for delivering me from the torture
of being argued with by the King's learned men, and I
knelt down several times.

An angel sent from God, and from none other, delivered the sign to my King. And I thanked God for it
again and again.

II

MONDAY, MARCH 12

*Was the angel who brought the sign the angel
who first appeared to you, or was it another?*
It is always one and the same. And he has never failed
me.

Has not the angel failed you in worldly things
in allowing you to be taken prisoner?
I believe, since it pleases our Lord, that it is best that I
am a prisoner.

Has he not failed you in the things of grace?
How can he have failed me, when he comforts me every
day? I mean by the comfort from Saint Catherine and
Saint Margaret.

Do you call them, or do they come without your calling?
They often come without my calling. And sometimes,
if they did not come quickly, I prayed our Lord to send
them.

Did you ever call them, and they did not come?
I have never had need of them and not had them.

When you promised our Lord to keep your virginity,
was it to him that you spoke?
It ought to be enough to promise it to those who were
sent by him, that is, Saint Catherine and Saint Margaret.

When you saw Saint Michael and the angels,
did you show them reverence?
Yes.

Were they with you long?
They often come among Christian people and are not
seen. I have seen them many times among Christians.

III

AFTERNOON OF THE SAME DAY

Did the voice bid you put on men's clothing?
Whatever I have done that was good, I have done at the
bidding of my voices.

Did you think you were doing wrong
to put on men's clothing?
No. And even now, if I were with the other side in this
clothing of a man, I think it would be one of the best of
things for France for me to do as I was doing before my
capture!

IV

The sign was what the angel declared to my King, bringing him the crown, and telling him that he would possess the whole Kingdom of France, entirely, by God's help and through my effort, and that he should set me to work—that is, give me soldiers—or he would nowhere near so soon be crowned and anointed.

It was in the King's chamber in the castle of Chinon. The day I do not know; as for the hour, it was far advanced—other than that I do not remember. It was in the month of April or March, I think, two years ago this coming April or else this present month. It was after Easter.

Of what material was the crown?
It is a good thing to know that it was of fine gold, and it was so rich that I could not tell its richness.

And the crown signified that he would hold the Kingdom of France.

Did you handle it or kiss it?
No.

Did the angel who brought it come from above,
or along the ground?
He came from above—I mean, he came at our Lord's
bidding. He entered by the door of the chamber.

Did he move along the ground from the door of the chamber?
When he came into the King's presence, he did him reverence, bowing before him and speaking the words I
have told you about the sign. Then he reminded him of
the beautiful patience he had shown in the face of the
great tribulations which had come to him. And from
the door of the chamber he stepped and moved along
the ground as he came to the King.

When the angel came I accompanied him and went
with him up the steps to the King's chamber, and the
angel went in first. And then I said to the King, "Sire,
there is your sign. Take it."

In what place did the angel appear to you?
I was almost always in prayer to the end that God might
send the King's sign. And I was in my lodging, which
was in the house of a good woman near the castle of
Chinon, when he came; and then we went together to
the King. And he was well accompanied by other angels
with him, whom everyone did not see.

Were you told where the angel obtained the crown?
It was brought, sent by God. There is no goldsmith on earth who could have made it so beautiful or so rich. As to where he obtained it, I leave that to God. I know nothing more of where it was obtained.

Did the crown have a good odor?
It smells good, and will. But it must be well kept, as befits it. It was in the fashion of a crown.

V

WEDNESDAY, MARCH 14

Do your voices ask you for time in which to answer?
Saint Catherine answers me at times. And sometimes I fail to understand because of the turmoil in the prisons and the noise made by my guards. When I appeal to Saint Catherine, immediately she and Saint Margaret appeal to our Lord, and then, as our Lord bids them, they give me answer.

There is no day that they do not come into this castle.

I have asked my voices for three things: one is my freedom; another, that God will help the French and watch over the towns that acknowledge them; and the other, my soul's salvation.

This was what I said to Monseigneur de Beauvais, and still is: "You say that you are my judge; I know not if you are. But look that you do not judge ill, because you would put yourself in great danger." And I give you this warning so that, if our Lord punishes you for it, my duty to tell you is done.

What is this danger?
Saint Catherine has told me that I shall have succour, and I do not know if it is to be that I shall be freed from my prison, or if when I am being sentenced there will be some disturbance there by means of which I could be freed. I think that it will be one or the other. Most often my voices tell me that I shall be freed by a great victory. And afterwards my voices say, "Accept all willingly, heed not your martyrdom, you shall come at last into the Kingdom of Paradise." And this my voices have told me simply and absolutely, that is, assuredly. I call it martyrdom because of the pain and oppression that I suffer in prison. I do not know if I shall suffer a greater; that I leave with our Lord.

I firmly believe what my voices have told me, which is that I shall be saved, as firmly as if I were already there.

That is an answer of great weight.
I hold it also to be a great treasure.

VI

AFTERNOON OF THE SAME DAY

As to my assurance of my salvation, about which I was questioned this morning, I meant: provided that I keep the oath and the promise which I made to our Lord— that is, to keep my virginity in body and soul.

Is there any need for you to confess, since you believe,
by the revelation of your voices, that you will be saved?
I do not know that I have sinned mortally. But I think that if I were in mortal sin Saint Catherine and Saint Margaret would abandon me at once. And to answer your question, I think that it is not possible to cleanse your conscience too often.

The evil thing that you did when you jumped
from the tower—do you think that was a mortal sin?
I do not know. I leave it to our Lord.

You wear men's clothing. Do you not think
that you have sinned mortally in doing that?
Since I do it at our Lord's bidding and in his service, I do not think I am doing wrong. And when he shall be pleased to direct, it shall be quickly laid aside.

VII

THURSDAY, MARCH 15

We admonish you: if you have done anything
contrary to our faith you must refer it
to the determination of the Church.

Let my answers be seen and examined by clerics, and
then let me be told if there is anything in them contrary
to the Christian faith. I shall know from my council
what to make of it and what to say, and then I will say
what I have learned from my council. But if in my answers there is any evil thing, contrary to the Christian
faith which our Lord has ordained, I should not want
to defend it, and I should be very sorry to go a contrary
way.

The difference between the Church militant and the Church
triumphant is explained to her. Then:

We appeal to you to submit now to the determination
of the Church in respect to what you have said
and done, whether good or evil.

I will not now answer you further on that.

Which would you rather do—put on women's clothing and
hear mass, or remain in men's clothing and not hear mass?
Assure me that I shall hear mass if I am in women's
clothing, and I will answer you.

I assure you of that.
And what do you say if I have sworn and promised our
King not to abandon this clothing? However, I answer
you: Have a dress made for me, long enough to reach
the ground and without a train, and give it to me to go
to mass in. And then, when I come back, I will dress
again in the clothing that I have on.

I carry out our Lord's command, given me by my
voices, with all my might—so much of it as I can understand. And they command me nothing save at our
Lord's good pleasure.

VIII

SATURDAY, MARCH 17

Will you submit yourself to the determination
of our mother, holy Church, in respect to all
your words and deeds, whether good or evil?
As for the Church, I love it and I would wish to support
it with all my might for the sake of our Christian faith:

it is not I who should be prevented from going to church and hearing mass! As for the good work I have done and my first coming, I must needs leave that with the King of Heaven, who sent me to Charles, son of Charles King of France, who shall be King. And you shall see that the French will very soon achieve a great task which God will send to the French, and such that almost the whole Kingdom of France will tremble. And I say it, so that when it comes to pass it will be remembered that I said it.

Answer whether you will refer yourself
to the determination of the Church?
I refer myself to our Lord who sent me, to Our Lady, and to all the blessed saints in Paradise. It seems to me that our Lord and the Church are one and the same, and that no one should make difficulties about that. Why do you make difficulties about its not being one and the same?

What do you say in regard to the women's clothing
that was offered you so that you might go to hear mass?
As to women's clothing, I will not have it yet, nor until it shall please our Lord. And if indeed I must be led out to the place of judgment, and if I must be unclothed in

the place of judgment, I beg the lords of the Church to allow me to have a woman's shift and a kerchief on my head. I would rather die than revoke what our Lord has caused me to do. And I firmly believe that our Lord will never permit me to be brought so low and not very quickly have succour from God and by a miracle.

Not for anything would I take an oath not to arm myself and wear men's clothing in order to do our Lord's pleasure!

Do you know that Saint Catherine
and Saint Margaret hate the English?
They love what God loves and hate what he hates.

Does God hate the English?
As to God's love or hate for the English, and what he will do to their souls, I know nothing. But I do know that they will be driven out of France, except those that die here, and that God will send the French victory over the English.

What support and what succour do you look to have
from our Lord in respect to your wearing men's clothing?
For that, as for the other things that I have done, I have not wished to have any other reward than the salvation of my soul.

IX

Did you ask your saints if, by virtue of your banner,
you would win every battle you entered, and be victorious?
They told me to take it up bravely and God would help
me.

Which helped the other more—you your banner,
or your banner you?
As to whether victory was my banner's or mine, it was
all our Lord's.

Should you consider yourself bound to tell
the whole truth to the Pope, God's vicar, in answer
to everything that you might be asked concerning
the faith and the state of your conscience?
Bring me before him, I beg you. And before him I will
answer whatever I ought.

X

Give me a woman's dress to go home to my mother in,
and I will take it. That would bring me out of prison,
and when I am out of prison I will take counsel over
what I should do.

Because of the solemnity of these days and this season, I beg to be permitted to hear mass on Palm Sunday.

XI

PALM SUNDAY, MARCH 25

I could well be allowed to hear mass as I am, which is my highest wish. But I cannot change my attire, nor does that lie in me.

It does not lie in me to do it. If it lay in me, it would be quickly done!

Re-Examination

I

IN THE ROOM OFF THE HALL OF STATE
TUESDAY, MARCH 27

First, for your admonishing me for my good and in our faith, I thank you and all this company. As for the counsellor that you offer me, I thank you too: but I do not intend to forsake the counsel of our Lord.

I believe that our holy father the Pope of Rome and the bishops and other churchmen are there to guard the Christian faith and to punish those who are faulty.

But as for me I will not submit myself in respect to my deeds, save to the church in Heaven alone—that is, to God, the Virgin Mary, and the saints in Paradise. And I firmly believe that I have not been faulty in our Christian faith. Nor would I wish to be.

I do not do wrong to serve God!

If the judges refuse to let me hear mass, it certainly lies in our Lord to let me hear it, when he shall please to, without them.

At Arras and at Beaurevoir I was many times admonished to wear women's clothing: I refused, and I still refuse. As to other womanly duties, there are enough other women to perform them.

As to the Duke of Burgundy, I begged him, by letters and through his ambassadors, that there might be peace. As to the English, the peace that is needed with them is that they should go back to their homes in England.

There was neither sorcery nor any other evil art in anything that I have done.

If the English had believed my letter they would have done wisely. And before seven years are ended, they shall be well aware of the things that I wrote to them.

I did not send it out of pride or presumption, but at the bidding of our Lord.

First I asked them to make peace. And in case they would not make peace, I was all ready to fight.

II

The gentlemen of France wanted to go before Paris. And I think they did their duty in that: it was going against their enemies.

It lies with our Lord to make revelations to whom he pleases.

As for signs, if those who ask for one are not worthy of it, I am not accountable for that!

I believe, as firmly as I believe that our Lord Jesus Christ suffered death to redeem us from the pains of Hell, that they are Saint Michael and Saint Gabriel and Saint Catherine and Saint Margaret, whom our Lord sends to comfort and counsel me.

I shall call them to help me as long as I live.

I ask in this manner:

"Most sweet God, in honor of your holy passion I

beg you, if you love me, to reveal to me what I am to answer to these churchmen. As to this clothing I well know by what commandment I began to wear it. But I do not know the manner in which I am to quit it. Therefore, may it please you to teach me."

And immediately they come.

That Jesus has failed me I deny.

As to the Church militant, I wish to show it all the honor and reverence that I can. As for referring my deeds to the Church militant, I must needs refer them to our Lord, who caused me to do what I have done.

I am a good Christian.

The offenses that you bring against me I have not committed: as for the rest, I refer it to our Lord.

III

IN HER PRISON
SATURDAY, MARCH 31

Will you refer yourself to the judgment of the Church
militant in respect to all that you have done, whether good
or evil, and particularly in respect to the acts, crimes,
and offenses which are imputed to you?

Concerning what you ask I will refer myself to the
Church militant, provided that it does not command
me to do anything impossible.

I call this impossible—that I should revoke the
things which I have said and done, as they are set down
in this trial, concerning the visions and revelations
which I have said that I had from God. Not for anything will I revoke them. And what our Lord has
caused and commanded me to do, and shall command,
I will not cease from doing for any man living. And it
would be impossible for me to revoke them. And in
case the Church wished to make me do something else,
contrary to the commandment which I say God has
given me, not for anything would I do it.

If the Church militant tells you that your revelations are
illusions or diabolical things or superstitions or evil things,
will you refer yourself to the Church in respect to them?
I will refer myself to our Lord, whose bidding I shall always do. And I know that what is recorded in my trial
came to pass at my Lord's bidding. And what I have af-
firmed at my trial that I did at God's bidding, it would
have been impossible for me to do otherwise.

Do you not believe that you are subject to the Church which
is on earth, that is, to our holy father the Pope, the cardinals,
archbishops, bishops, and other prelates of the Church?
Yes—our Lord first served!

Have you a command from your voices not to submit
yourself to the Church militant, which is on earth,
or to its judgment?
What I answer is not whatever comes into my head.
What I answer is at their command. They do not command me not to obey the Church, our Lord first served!

Lying Sick in Prison, She is Visited and Exhorted by the Judges

WEDNESDAY, APRIL 18

You have been questioned concerning great and difficult matters, and it seems that in many things you have erred. But because you are an unlettered and ignorant woman, unable to discern whether such things are contrary to our faith, we offer you a good counsellor to advise you. Choose one or more from among those here, to counsel you: they are doctors of theology and of canon and civil law. But if you will not accept counsel and do as the Church counsels you, you are in great danger.

I think, for the sickness I have, that I am in great danger of death. And if so it be that God is pleased to do his will to me, I pray you that I may have confession, and my Saviour too, and that I may be buried in consecrated ground.

If my body dies in prison, I trust to you to have it laid in consecrated ground. If you do not, I entrust it to our Lord.

Whatever it may bring to me, I will neither do nor say anything more than I have already said that I would at this trial.

She is Publicly Admonished

IN THE ROOM OFF THE HALL OF STATE
WEDNESDAY, MAY 2

Read on, and then I will answer you. I look to God, my creator, in all. I love him with all my heart.

Is that all that you wish to answer now?
I look to my judge—he is King of Heaven and earth.

Do you mean to say that you have no judge on this earth?
Is not our holy father the Pope your judge?
I will not answer further to that. I have a good master— that is, our Lord—to whom only I look, and to none other.

When I shall have done that for which I am sent from God, I will put on women's clothing.

You will not do what you say against me without suffering for it both in body and soul.

She is Threatened with Torture
in the Presence of the Instruments

DONJON OF THE CASTLE
WEDNESDAY, MAY 9

Truly, if you were to have me torn limb from limb and send my soul out of my body, I would say nothing else. And if I did say anything, afterwards I should always say that you had made me say it by force.

I have asked my voices to counsel me whether I should submit to the Church, because the churchmen were pressing me to submit to the Church. And my voices have told me that, if I want our Lord to help me, I must lay all my deeds before him.

Last Session: She is Again Admonished

WEDNESDAY, MAY 23

If I were at the place of execution, and I saw the fire lighted, and the faggots catching and the executioner ready to build up the fire, and if I were in the fire, even so I would say nothing else, and I would maintain what I have said at this trial until death.

I have nothing more to say.

The First Sentence

Thursday, May 24

Cemetery of Saint-Ouen

SHE IS PUBLICLY PREACHED TO

Speak not against my King! He is a good Christian.

SHE IS REPEATEDLY PRESSED TO RECANT

You take great pains to seduce me.

I leave it to your consciences whether I should recant or not.

THE BISHOP BEGINS TO READ HER SENTENCE;
A WRITTEN FORM OF ABJURATION IS
PRESENTED TO HER

I am content to do what you will have me.

I would rather sign it than burn.

Now, you churchmen, take me to your prison, and let me be no longer in the hands of the English.

She Revokes Her Abjuration

Monday, May 28

In Her Prison

W<small>HAT I SAID</small>, I said for fear of the fire.

My voices have told me since that I did a very wicked thing in confessing that what I had done was not well done.

They told me that God, by Saint Catherine and Saint Margaret, gave me to know the great pity of the treason that I consented to by making that abjuration and revocation to save my life, and that I was damning myself to save my life.

If I should say that God had not sent me, I should damn myself. It is true that God has sent me.

Last Day

Wednesday, May 30

In Her Prison: Early Morning

I T WAS I who brought the message of the crown to my King. I was the angel and there was no other. And the crown was no more than the promise of my King's coronation, which I made to him.

Alas! Am I so horribly and cruelly used, that my clean body, never yet defiled, must this day be burnt and turn to ashes! Ha! Ha! I would rather be beheaded seven times than suffer burning.

Alas! If I had been kept in the Church's prison, to which I had submitted—if I had been kept by churchmen, instead of by my enemies and adversaries, I should not have come to such a miserable end. Oh, I appeal to God, the great judge, from this great wrong and oppression!

Bishop, I die through you!

Master Peter, where shall I be this night? By God's grace I shall be in Paradise.

She is Led to the Place of Execution

Rouen, Rouen, shalt thou be my dwelling?

I beg each priest here to say a mass for me.

At the Stake

I pray you, go to the nearest church, and bring me the cross, and hold it up level with my eyes until I am dead. I would have the cross on which God hung be ever before my eyes while life lasts in me.

Jesus, Jesus!

Notes on the Text

Sources

With the one exception noted below, all the *narrative passages* are from Joan's own testimony at her trial.

The greater number of the *interpolated speeches* are derived from the depositions of the persons to whom they were addressed. The greater number of those which are not so derived—notably the speeches to King Charles, who did not testify for the rehabilitation proceedings—are from the testimony of bystanders. The rest are from the more reliable chronicles.

The questions and answers of the *trial scenes* are, of course, from the Trial itself.

Joan's words on the day of the *First Sentence* and on her *Last Day* are from the depositions of those who were best placed to hear her on those occasions.

Treatment

In handling the material I have taken only these liberties:

1. That of restoring passages of indirect discourse to their direct form.

2. That of bringing together passages of the trial testimony separated in the telling but dealing with one subject.

3. That of replacing a pronoun by its antecedent.

4. That of condensing the more prolix of the questions and exhortations addressed to Joan by the judges.

Dates

The dates are those which are generally accepted. Most of them are well established. Those about which there is any important difference of opinion are noted below.

Notes

Page 1. "1412"—the year of Joan's birth is not known with certainty.

Page 5. "Polled Wood"—so translated in an attempt to render the equivoque of the original *Bois-chesnu*, which may mean either "oak wood" or "gray-haired wood."

Page 9. "February, 1429"—some authorities place this departure in January or in December; some also hold that an abortive attempt preceded the actual departure by several months.

Page 15. "Is not the Dauphin's" and "have the Kingdom in custody"—originals, *non spectabat Dalphino* and *haberet in commendam*, feudal terms which I have paraphrased.

Page 26. "I was ill content," etc.—This and the following paragraph constitute the narrative passage referred to above as derived from a source other than Joan's own testimony.

They are from the deposition of her chaplain, who quotes them as part of the account she gave him of events prior to their acquaintance.

Page 28. "Uphold the blood royal"—original, *réclamer le sanc royal*. By some held to refer to the imprisonment of the Duke of Orléans, in which case *réclamer* means "redeem." I am inclined to think otherwise, and have translated accordingly.

Page 29. "Hand to hand"—original, *corps pour corps*, an expression commonly used in reference to a formal combat in which specified equal numbers fight on either side. As it is one of the expressions which Joan denied having used, the determination of its precise meaning here is of little importance. For her denial, reference may be made to page 102.

Page 35. "Follow them"—reading *eos* for *eam*.

Page 63. "He is to surrender . . . to him"—"he" stands for the Duke; "him," for the King. I have punctuated this letter differently from the editions I have seen, in an effort to bring out what I conceive to be the parallel use of the conjunctions *combien que* and *combien aussi que*.

Page 77. "To my . . . town of Reims"—omitting *maistres*, which has no precise meaning in this context.

Page 90. "I ask him" etc.—from the Trial, but vouched for only by the messenger, the clerks of court not having been present.

Page 91. "The Trial"—the autobiographical passages of the Trial having already made their appearance, they are not repeated here. Excluded with them are passages merely routine or merely repetitions and those in which subjects are touched on but not developed. It has not seemed practicable to indicate these omissions in the text.

Page 102. "Spoke that letter"—i.e., dictated it.

Page 111. "The King's learned men"—original, *clercs de par delà,* i.e., "yonder," implying party as well as place.

Page 122. "Revoke"—original, *revoquer.* It may safely be assumed that this word did not form part of Joan's natural vocabulary; in using it, she seems to have had in mind its general nature rather than its strict meaning. Another example may be found on page 128.

Acknowledgments

No student of Joan of Arc can feel anything but the deepest gratitude to the great Jules Quicherat, whose *Procès de condamnation et de réhabilitation de Jeanne d'Arc . . . suivis de . . . documents historiques* (Paris, 1841–1849) contains not only the two trials but a large amount of supplementary material; and to his distinguished successor, M. Pierre Champion, for his *Procès de condamnation de Jeanne d'Arc. Texte, traduction et notes* (Paris, 1920–1921). It is upon their editorial labors that I have chiefly based my text. Since Quicherat's time, the originals of three of Joan's letters have been published by M. le comte de Maleissye. For my special purpose I have had little occasion to consult the host of those who have devoted themselves to clearing up particular moments of Joan's career or to disinterring minor documents. Yet such labors make themselves felt, even if only indirectly. Joseph Fabre, in his dramatic versions of the two *Trials* (Paris, 1884 and 1888), was, I believe, the first to restore life to the third-person narrative by substituting the first person, a procedure in which he has had many followers. My principal guide to the succession of events has been the *Itinéraire de la Pucelle* published in Quicherat's fifth volume.

Afterword

(1851)

Sir Edward S. Creasy

The eyes of all Europe were turned towards this scene, where, it was reasonably supposed, the French were to make their last stand for maintaining the independence of their monarchy and the rights of their sovereign.   HUME

When, after their victory at Salamis, the generals of the various Greek states voted the prizes for distinguished individual merit, each assigned the first place of excellence to himself, but they all concurred in giving their second votes to Themistocles. This was looked on as a decisive proof that Themistocles ought to be ranked first of all. If we were to endeavour, by a similar test, to ascertain which European nation has contributed the most to the progress of European civilisation, we should find Italy, Germany, England, and Spain, each claiming the first degree, but each also naming France as clearly next in merit. It is impossible to deny her paramount importance in history. Besides the formidable part that she has for nearly three centuries played, as the Bellona of the European commonwealth of states, her influence during all this period over the arts, the literature, the manners and the feelings of mankind, has been such as to make the crisis of her earlier fortunes a point of worldwide interest; and it may be asserted without exaggeration, that the future career of every nation was involved in the result of the struggle, by which the unconscious heroine of France, in the beginning of the fifteenth century, rescued her country from becoming a second Ireland under the yoke of the triumphant English.

Seldom has the extinction of a nation's independence appeared more inevitable than was the case in France, when the English invaders completed their lines round Orleans, four hundred and twenty-three years ago. A series of dreadful defeats had thinned the chivalry of France, and daunted the spirits of her soldiers. A foreign king had been proclaimed in her capital; and foreign armies of the bravest veterans, and led by the ablest captains then known in the world, occupied the fairest portions of her territory. Worse to her, even than the fierceness and the strength of her foes, were the factions, the vices, and the crimes of her own children. Her native prince was a dissolute trifler, stained with the assassination of the most powerful noble of the land, whose son, in revenge, had leagued himself with the enemy. Many more of her nobility, many of her prelates, her magistrates, and rulers, had sworn fealty to the English king. The condition of the peasantry amid the general prevalence of anarchy and brigandage, which were added to the customary devastations of contending armies, was wretched beyond the power of language to describe. The sense of terror and suffering seemed to have extended itself even to the brute creation.

"In sooth, the estate of France was then most miserable. There appeared nothing but a horrible face, confusion, poverty, desolation, solitarinesse, and feare. The lean and bare labourers in the country did terrifie even theeves themselves, who had nothing left them to spoile but the carkasses of these poore miserable creatures, wandering up and down like ghostes drawne out of their graves. The least farmes and hamlets were fortified by these robbers, English, Bourguegnons, and French, every one striving to do his worst; all men-of-war were well agreed to spoile the countryman and merchant. *Even the cattell, accustomed to the larume bell, the signe of the enemy's approach, would run home of themselves without any guide, by this accustomed misery.*"[1]

In the autumn of 1428, the English, who were already masters of all France north of the Loire, prepared their forces for the conquest of the southern provinces, which yet adhered to the cause of the dauphin. The city of Orleans, on the banks of that river, was looked upon as the last stronghold of the French national party. If the English could once obtain possession of it, their victorious progress through the residue of the kingdom seemed free from any serious obstacle. Accordingly, the Earl of Salisbury, one of the bravest and most experienced of the English generals, who had been trained under Henry V, marched to the attack of the all-important city; and, after reducing several places of inferior consequence in the neighbourhood, appeared with his army before its walls on the 12th of October 1428.

The city of Orleans itself was on the north side of the Loire, but its suburbs extended far on the southern side, and a strong bridge connected them with the

[1]De Serres, quoted in the notes to Southey's *Joan of Arc*.

town. A fortification which in modern military phrase would be termed a tête-du-pont, defended the bridge-head on the southern side, and two towers, called the Tourelles, were built on the bridge itself, where it rested on an island at a little distance from the tête-du-pont. Indeed, the solid masonry of the bridge terminated at the Tourelles; and the communication thence with the tête-du-pont on the southern shore was by means of a drawbridge. The Tourelles and the tête-du-pont formed together a strong fortified post, capable of containing a garrison of considerable strength, and so long as this was in possession of the Orleannais, they could communicate freely with the southern provinces, the inhabitants of which, like the Orleannais themselves, supported the cause of their Dauphin against the foreigners. Lord Salisbury rightly judged the capture of the Tourelles to be the most material step towards the reduction of the city itself. Accordingly he directed his principal operations against this post, and after some severe repulses, he carried the Tourelles by storm, on the 23rd of October. The French, however, broke down the part of the bridge which was nearest to the north bank, and thus rendered a direct assault from the Tourelles upon the city impossible. But the possession of this post enabled the English to distress the town greatly by a battery of cannon which they planted there, and which commanded some of the principal streets.

It has been observed by Hume that this is the first siege in which any important use appears to have been made of artillery. And even at Orleans both besiegers and besieged seem to have employed their cannons more as instruments of destruction against their enemy's *men*, than as engines of demolition against their enemy's walls and works. The efficacy of cannon in breaching solid masonry was taught Europe by the Turks, a few years afterwards, at the memorable siege of Constantinople. In our French wars, as in the wars of the classic nations, famine was looked on as the surest weapon to compel the submission of a well-walled town; and the great object of the besiegers was to effect a complete circumvallation. The great ambit of the walls of Orleans, and the facilities which the river gave for obtaining succour and supplies, rendered the capture of the place by this process a matter of great difficulty. Nevertheless, Lord Salisbury, and Lord Suffolk, who succeeded him in command of the English after his death by a cannon-ball, carried on the necessary works with great skill and resolution. Six strongly-fortified posts, called bastilles, were formed at certain intervals round the town; and the purpose of the English engineers was to draw strong lines between them. During the winter little progress was made with the entrenchments, but when the spring of 1429 came, the English resumed their works with activity; the communications between the city and the country became more difficult, and the approach of want began already to be felt in Orleans.

The besieging force also fared hardly for stores and provisions, until relieved by the effects of a brilliant victory which Sir John Fastolfe, one of the best English generals, gained at Rouvrai, near Orleans, a few days after Ash Wednesday 1429. With only sixteen hundred fighting men, Sir John completely defeated an army of French and Scots, four thousand strong, which had been collected for the purpose of aiding the Orleannais, and harassing the besiegers. After this encounter, which seemed decisively to confirm the superiority of the English in battle over their adversaries, Fastolfe escorted large supplies of stores and food to Suffolk's camp, and the spirits of the English rose to the highest pitch at the prospect of the speedy capture of the city before them; and the consequent subjection of all France beneath their arms.

The Orleannais now in their distress offered to surrender the city into the hands of the Duke of Burgundy, who, though the ally of the English, was yet one of their native princes. The Regent Bedford refused these terms, and the speedy submission of the city to the English seemed inevitable. The Dauphin Charles, who was now at Chinon with his remnant of a court, despaired of maintaining any longer the struggle for his crown; and was only prevented from abandoning the country by the more masculine spirits of his mistress and his queen. Yet neither they, nor the boldest of Charles's captains, could have shown him where to find resources for prolonging the war; and least of all, could any human skill have predicted the quarter whence rescue was to come to Orleans and to France.

In the village of Domremy, on the borders of Lorraine, there was a poor peasant of the name of Jacques d'Arc, respected in his station of life, and who had reared a family in virtuous habits and in the practice of the strictest devotion. His eldest daughter was named by her parents Jeannette, but she was called Jeanne by the French, which was Latinised into Johanna, and Anglicised into Joan.

At the time when Joan first attracted attention, she was about eighteen years of age. She was naturally of a

susceptible disposition, which diligent attention to the
legends of saints, and tales of fairies, aided by the
dreamy loneliness of her life while tending her father's
flocks[2] had made peculiarly prone to enthusiastic fer-

[2]Southey, in one of the speeches which he puts in the mouth of his
Joan of Arc, has made her beautifully describe the effect on her mind
of the scenery in which she dwelt:

> "Here in solitude and peace
> My soul was nurst, amid the loveliest scenes
> Of unpolluted nature. Sweet it was
> As the white mists of morning roll'd away,
> To see the mountain's wooded heights appear
> Dark in the early dawn, and mark its slope
> With gorse-flowers glowing, as the rising sun
> On the golden ripeness pour'd a deepening light.
> Pleasant at noon beside the vocal brook
> To lay me down, and watch the floating clouds,
> And shape to Fancy's wild similitudes
> Their ever-varying forms; and oh, how sweet,
> To drive my flock at evening to the fold,
> And hasten to our little hut, and hear
> The voice of kindness bid me welcome home!"

The only foundation for the story told by the Burgundian partisan
Monstrelet, and adopted by Hume, of Joan having been brought up
as servant at an inn, is the circumstance of her having been once, with
the rest of her family, obliged to take refuge in an *auberge* in Neufchâteau for fifteen days, when a party of Burgundian cavalry made
an incursion into Domremy.

vour. At the same time she was eminent for piety and purity of soul, and for her compassionate gentleness to the sick and the distressed.

The district where she dwelt had escaped comparatively free from the ravages of war, but the approach of roving bands of Burgundian or English troops frequently spread terror through Domremy. Once the village had been plundered by some of these marauders, and Joan and her family had been driven from their home, and forced to seek refuge for a time at Neufchâteau. The peasantry in Domremy were principally attached to the house of Orleans and the dauphin; and all the miseries which France endured, were there imputed to the Burgundian faction and their allies, the English, who were seeking to enslave unhappy France.

Thus from infancy to girlhood, Joan had heard continually of the woes of the war, and she had herself witnessed some of the wretchedness that it caused. A feeling of intense patriotism grew in her with her growth. The deliverance of France from the English was the subject of her reveries by day and her dreams by night. Blended with these aspirations were recollections of the miraculous interpositions of Heaven in favour of the oppressed, which she had learned from the legends of her church. Her faith was undoubting; her prayers were fervent. "She feared no danger, for she felt no sin"; and at length she believed herself to have received the supernatural inspiration which she sought.

According to her own narrative, delivered by her to her merciless inquisitors, in the time of her captivity and approaching death, she was about thirteen years old when her revelations commenced. Her own words describe them best.[3] "At the age of thirteen, a voice from God came near to her to help her in ruling herself, and that voice came to her about the hour of noon, in summer time, while she was in her father's garden. And she had fasted the day before. And she heard the voice on her right, in the direction of the church; and when she heard the voice she also saw a bright light. Afterwards, St. Michael and St. Margaret and St. Catherine appeared to her. They were always in a halo of glory; she could see that their heads were crowned with jewels: and she heard their voices, which were sweet and mild. She did not distinguish their arms or limbs. She heard them more frequently than she saw them; and the usual time when she heard them was when the church bells were sounding for prayer. And if she was in the woods when she heard them, she could plainly distinguish their voices drawing near to her. When she

[3] *Procès de Jeanne d'Arc.*

thought that she discerned the Heavenly Voices, she knelt down, and bowed herself to the ground. Their presence gladdened her even to tears; and after they departed she wept because they had not taken her with them back to Paradise. They always spoke soothingly to her. They told her that France would be saved, and that she was to save it." Such were the visions and the Voices that moved the spirit of the girl of thirteen; and as she grew older they became more frequent and more clear.

At last the tidings of the siege of Orleans reached Domremy. Joan heard her parents and neighbours talk of the sufferings of its population, of the ruin which its capture would bring on their lawful sovereign, and of the distress of the dauphin and his court. Joan's heart was sorely troubled at the thought of the fate of Orleans; and her Voices now ordered her to leave her home; and warned her that she was the instrument chosen by Heaven for driving away the English from that city, and for taking the dauphin to be anointed king at Rheims. At length she informed her parents of her divine mission, and told them that she must go to the Sire de Baudricourt, who commanded at Vaucouleurs, and who was the appointed person to bring her into the presence of the king, whom she was to save.

Neither the anger nor the grief of her parents, who said that they would rather see her drowned than exposed to the contamination of the camp, could move her from her purpose. One of her uncles consented to take her to Vaucouleurs, where De Baudricourt at first thought her mad, and derided her; but by degrees was led to believe, if not in her inspiration, at least in her enthusiasm, and in its possible utility to the dauphin's cause.

The inhabitants of Vaucouleurs were completely won over to her side by the piety and devoutness which she displayed, and by her firm assurance in the truth of her mission. She told them that it was God's will that she should go to the king, and that no one but her could save the kingdom of France. She said that she herself would rather remain with her poor mother and spin; but the Lord had ordered her forth. The fame of "the Maid," as she was termed, the renown of her holiness, and of her mission, spread far and wide. Baudricourt sent her with an escort to Chinon, where the Dauphin Charles was dallying away his time. Her Voices had bidden her assume the arms and the apparel of a knight; and the wealthiest inhabitants of Vaucouleurs had vied with each other in equipping her with war-horse, armour, and sword. On reaching Chinon, she was, after some delay, admitted into the presence of the dauphin. Charles designedly dressed himself far less richly than many of his courtiers were apparelled, and mingled with them, when Joan was introduced, in order to see if the Holy Maid would address her exhortations to the wrong person. But she instantly singled him out, and kneeling before him, said, "Most noble dauphin, the King of Heaven announces to you by me, that you shall be anointed and crowned king in the city of Rheims, and that you shall be his viceregent in France." His features may probably have been seen by her previously in portraits, or have been described to her by others; but she herself believed that her Voices inspired her when she addressed the king; and the report soon spread abroad that the Holy Maid had found the king by a miracle; and this, with many other similar rumours, augmented the renown and influence that she now rapidly acquired.

The state of public feeling in France was now favourable to an enthusiastic belief in a Divine interposition in favour of the party that had hitherto been unsuccessful and oppressed. The humiliations which had befallen the French royal family and nobility were looked on as the just judgments of God upon them for their vice and impiety. The misfortunes that had come upon France as a nation were believed to have been drawn down by national sins. The English, who had been the instruments of Heaven's wrath against France, seemed now by their pride and cruelty to be fitting objects of it themselves. France in that age was a profoundly religious country. There was ignorance, there was superstition, there was bigotry; but there was Faith—a Faith that itself worked true miracles, even while it believed in unreal ones. At this time, also, one of those devotional movements began among the clergy in France, which from time to time occur in national churches, without it being possible for the historian to assign any adequate human cause for their immediate date or extension. Numberless friars and priests traversed the rural districts and towns of France, preaching to the people that they must seek from Heaven a deliverance from the pillages of the soldiery and the insolence of the foreign oppressors. The idea of a Providence that works only by general laws was wholly alien to the feelings of the age. Every political event, as well as every natural phenomenon, was believed to be the immediate result of a special mandate of God. This led to the belief that his holy angels and saints were constantly employed in executing his commands and mingling in the affairs of men. The church encouraged these feelings; and at the same time sanctioned the concurrent popular belief that hosts of evil spirits were also ever actively interposing in the current of earthly events, with whom sorcerers and wizards could league themselves, and thereby obtain the exercise of supernatural power.

Thus all things favoured the influence which Joan obtained both over friends and foes. The French nation, as well as the English and the Burgundians, readily admitted that superhuman beings inspired her: the only question was, whether these beings were good or evil angels; whether she brought with her "airs from heaven, or blasts from hell." This question seemed to her countrymen to be decisively settled in her favour, by the austere sanctity of her life, by the holiness of her conversation, but, still more by her exemplary attention to all the services and rites of the church. The dauphin at first feared the injury that might be done to his cause if he had laid himself open to the charge of having leagued himself with a sorceress. Every imaginable test, therefore, was resorted to in order to set Joan's orthodoxy and purity beyond suspicion. At last, Charles and his advisers felt safe in accepting her services as those of a true and virtuous Christian daughter of the Holy Church.

It is indeed probable that Charles himself and some of his counsellors may have suspected Joan of being a mere enthusiast; and it is certain that Dunois, and others of the best generals, took considerable latitude in obeying or deviating from the military orders that she gave. But over the mass of the people and the soldiery, her influence was unbounded. While Charles and his doctors of theology, and court ladies, had been deliberating as to recognising or dismissing the Maid, a considerable period had passed away, during which a small army, the last gleanings, as it seemed, of the English sword, had been assembled at Blois, under Dunois, La Hire, Xaintrailles, and other chiefs, who to their natural valour were now beginning to unite the wisdom that is taught by misfortune. It was resolved to send Joan with this force and a convoy of provisions to Orleans. The distress of that city had now become urgent. But the communication with the open country was not entirely cut off: the Orleannais had heard of the Holy Maid whom Providence had raised up for their deliverance, and their messengers urgently implored the dauphin to send her to them without delay.

Joan appeared at the camp at Blois, clad in a new suit of brilliant white armour, mounted on a stately black war-horse, and with a lance in her right hand, which she had learned to wield with skill and grace. Her head was unhelmeted; so that all could behold her fair and expressive features, her deep-set and earnest eyes, and her long black hair, which was parted across her forehead, and bound by a ribbon behind her back. She wore at her side a small battle-axe, and the consecrated sword, marked on the blade with five crosses, which had at her bidding been taken for her from the shrine of St. Catherine at Fierbois. A page carried her banner, which she had caused to be made and embroidered as her Voices enjoined. It was white satin, strewn with fleurs-de-lis; and on it were the words "JHESUS MARIA," and the representation of the Saviour in His glory. Joan afterwards generally bore her banner herself in battle; she said that though she loved her sword much, she loved her banner forty times as much; and she loved to carry it because it could not kill any one.

Thus accoutred, she came to lead the troops of France, who looked with soldierly admiration on her well-proportioned and upright figure, the skill with which she managed her war-horse, and the easy grace with which she handled her weapons. Her military education had been short, but she had availed herself of it well. She had also the good sense to interfere little with the manœuvres of the troops: leaving those things to Dunois, and others whom she had the discernment to recognise as the best officers in the camp. Her tactics in action were simple enough. As she herself described it— "I used to say to them, 'Go boldly in among the English,' and then I used to go in boldly myself."[4] Such, as she told her inquisitors, was the only spell she used; and it was one of power. But while interfering little with the military discipline of the troops, in all matters of moral discipline she was inflexibly strict. All the abandoned followers of the camp were driven away. She compelled both generals and soldiers to attend regularly at confessional. Her chaplain and other priests marched with the army under her orders; and at every halt, an altar was set up and the sacrament administered. No oath or foul language passed without punishment or censure. Even the roughest and most hardened veterans obeyed her. They put off for a time the bestial coarseness which had grown on them during a life of bloodshed and rapine; they felt that they must go forth in a new spirit to a new career, and acknowledged the beauty of the holiness in which the Heaven-sent Maid was leading them to certain victory.

Joan marched from Blois on the 25th of April with a convoy of provisions for Orleans, accompanied by Dunois, La Hire, and the other chief captains of the French; and on the evening of the 28th they ap-

[4]*Procès de Jeanne d'Arc.*

proached the town. In the words of the old chronicler Hall: "The Englishmen, perceiving that they within could not long continue for faute of vitaile and pouder, kept not their watche so diligently as thei were accustomed, nor scoured now the countrey environed as their before had ordained. Whiche negligence the citizens shut in perceiving, sent worde thereof to the French captaines, which with Pucelle in the dedde tyme of the nighte, and in a greate rayne and thundere, with all their vitaile and artillery entered into the citie."

When it was day, the Maid rode in solemn procession through the city, clad in complete armour, and mounted on a white horse. Dunois was by her side, and all the bravest knights of her army and of the garrison followed in her train. The whole population thronged around her; and men, women, and children strove to touch her garments, or her banner, or her charger. They poured forth blessings on her, whom they already considered their deliverer. In the words used by two of them afterwards before the tribunal, which reversed the sentence, but could not restore the life of the Virgin-martyr of France, "the people of Orleans, when they first saw her in their city, thought that it was an angel from heaven that had come down to save them." Joan spoke gently in reply to their acclamations and addresses. She told them to fear God, and trust in Him for safety from the fury of their enemies. She first went to the principal church, where *Te Deum* was chanted; and then she took up her abode in the house of Jacques Bourgier, one of the principal citizens, and whose wife was a matron of good repute. She refused to attend a splendid banquet which had been provided for her, and passed nearly all her time in prayer.

When it was known by the English that the Maid was in Orleans, their minds were not less occupied about her than were the minds of those in the city; but it was in a very different spirit. The English believed in her supernatural mission as firmly as the French did; but they thought her a sorceress who had come to overthrow them by her enchantments. An old prophecy, which told that a damsel from Lorraine was to save France, had long been current; and it was known and applied to Joan by foreigners as well as by the natives. For months the English had heard of the coming Maid; and the tales of miracles which she was said to have wrought had been listened to by the rough yeomen of the English camp with anxious curiosity and secret awe. She had sent a herald to the English generals before she marched for Orleans; and he had summoned the English generals in the name of the Most High to

give up to the Maid, who was sent by Heaven, the keys
of the French cities which they had wrongfully taken:
and he also solemnly adjured the English troops,
whether archers, or men of the companies of war, or
gentlemen, or others, who were before the city of Orleans, to depart thence to their homes, under peril of
being visited by the judgment of God. On her arrival in
Orleans, Joan sent another similar message; but the
English scoffed at her from their towers, and threat-
ened to burn her heralds. She determined before she
shed the blood of the besiegers, to repeat the warning with her own voice; and accordingly she mounted
one of the boulevards of the town, which was within
hearing of the Tourelles; and thence she spoke to the
English, and bade them depart, otherwise they would
meet with shame and woe.

Sir William Gladsdale (whom the French call *Glacidas*) commanded the English post at the Tourelles, and
he and another English officer replied by bidding her go
home and keep her cows, and by ribald jests, that
brought tears of shame and indignation into her eyes.
But though the English leaders vaunted aloud, the effect produced on their army by Joan's presence in Orleans was proved four days after her arrival; when, on
the approach of reinforcements and stores to the town,

Joan and La Hire marched out to meet them, and escorted the long train of provision waggons safely into Orleans, between the bastilles of the English, who cowered behind their walls, instead of charging fiercely and fearlessly, as had been their wont, on any French band that dared to show itself within reach.

Thus far she had prevailed without striking a blow; but the time was now come to test her courage amid the horrors of actual slaughter. On the afternoon of the day on which she had escorted the reinforcements into the city, while she was resting fatigued at home, Dunois had seized an advantageous opportunity of attacking the English bastille of St. Loup: and a fierce assault of the Orleannais had been made on it, which the English garrison of the fort stubbornly resisted. Joan was roused by a sound which she believed to be that of her Heavenly Voices; she called for her arms and horse, and quickly equipping herself she mounted to ride off to where the fight was raging. In her haste she had forgotten her banner; she rode back, and, without dismounting, had it given to her from the window, and then she galloped to the gate, whence the sally had been made. On her way she met some of the wounded French who had been carried back from the fight. "Ha," she exclaimed, "I never can see French blood flow, without my hair standing on end." She rode out of the gate, and met the tide of her countrymen, who had been repulsed from the English fort, and were flying back to Orleans in confusion. At the sight of the Holy Maid and her banner they rallied, and renewed the assault. Joan rode forward at their head, waving her banner and cheering them on. The English quailed at what they believed to be the charge of hell; St. Loup was stormed, and its defenders put to the sword, except some few, whom Joan succeeded in saving. All her woman's gentleness returned when the combat was over. It was the first time that she had ever seen a battlefield. She wept at the sight of so many blood-stained and mangled corpses; and her tears flowed doubly when she reflected that they were the bodies of Christian men who had died without confession.

The next day was Ascension-day, and it was passed by Joan in prayer. But on the following morrow it was resolved by the chiefs of the garrison to attack the English forts on the south of the river. For this purpose they crossed the river in boats, and after some severe fighting, in which the Maid was wounded in the heel, both the English bastilles of the Augustins and St. Jean de Blanc were captured. The Tourelles were now the only post which the besiegers held on the south of the river. But that post was formidably strong, and by its command of the bridge, it was the key to the deliverance of Orleans. It was known that a fresh English army was approaching under Fastolfe to reinforce the besiegers, and should that army arrive, while the Tourelles were yet in the possession of their comrades, there was great peril of all the advantages which the French had gained being nullified, and of the siege being again actively carried on.

It was resolved, therefore, by the French, to assail the Tourelles at once, while the enthusiasm which the presence and the heroic valour of the Maid had created was at its height. But the enterprise was difficult. The rampart of the tête-du-pont, or landward bulwark, of the Tourelles was steep and high; and Sir William Gladsdale occupied this all-important fort with five hundred archers and men-at-arms, who were the very flower of the English army.

Early in the morning of the 7th of May, some thousands of the best French troops in Orleans heard Mass and attended the confessional by Joan's orders; and then crossing the river in boats, as on the preceding day, they assailed the bulwark of the Tourelles, "with light hearts and heavy hands." But Gladsdale's men, encouraged by their bold and skilful leader, made a resolute and able defence. The Maid planted her banner on the edge of the fosse, and then springing down into the ditch, she placed the first ladder against the wall, and began to mount. An English archer sent an arrow at her, which pierced her corselet and wounded her severely between the neck and shoulder. She fell bleeding from the ladder; and the English were leaping down from the wall to capture her, but her followers bore her off. She was carried to the rear, and laid upon the grass; her armour was taken off, and the anguish of her wound and the sight of her blood, made her at first tremble and weep. But her confidence in her celestial mission soon returned: her patron saints seemed to stand before her, and reassure her. She sat up and drew the arrow out with her own hands. Some of the soldiers who stood by wished to stanch the blood by saying a charm over the wound; but she forbade them, saying that she did not wish to be cured by unhallowed means. She had the wound dressed with a little oil, and then bidding her confessor come to her, she betook herself to prayer.

In the meanwhile, the English in the bulwark of the Tourelles had repulsed the oft-renewed efforts of the French to scale the wall. Dunois, who commanded the assailants, was at last discouraged, and gave orders for a retreat to be sounded. Joan sent for him and the other generals, and implored them not to despair. "By my God," she said to them, "you shall soon enter in there. Do not doubt it. When you see my banner wave again up to the wall, to your arms again! the fort is yours. For the present, rest a little, and take some food and drink." "They did so," says the old chronicler of the siege,[5] "for they obeyed her marvellously." The faintness caused by her wound had now passed off, and she headed the French in another rush against the bulwark. The English, who had thought her slain, were alarmed at her reappearance; while the French pressed furiously and fanatically forward. A Biscayan soldier was carrying Joan's banner. She had told the troops that directly the banner touched the wall they should enter. The Biscayan waved the banner forward from the edge of the fosse, and touched the wall with it; and then all the French host swarmed madly up the ladders that now were raised in all directions against the English fort. At this crisis, the efforts of the English garrison were distracted by an attack from another quarter. The French troops who had been left in Orleans had placed some planks over the broken part of the bridge, and advanced across them to the assault of the Tourelles on the

[5] *Journal du Siège d'Orléans.*

northern side. Gladsdale resolved to withdraw his men from the landward bulwark, and concentrate his whole force in the Tourelles themselves. He was passing for this purpose across the drawbridge that connected the Tourelles and the tête-du-pont, when Joan, who by this time had scaled the wall of the bulwark, called out to him, "Surrender, surrender to the King of Heaven. Ah, Glacidas, you have foully wronged me with your words, but I have great pity on your soul and the souls of your men." The Englishman, disdainful of her summons, was striding on across the drawbridge, when a cannon-shot from the town carried it away, and Gladsdale perished in the water than ran beneath. After his fall, the remnant of the English abandoned all further resistance. Three hundred of them had been killed in the battle, and two hundred were made prisoners.

DATE DUE			
MAR 1 9 1999			
OCT 1 7 2000			
MAR 1 5 2003			